Remain.

Meditation Guide &

Reflection Journal

Welcome to Remain!

We are so glad you are here. This is an opportunity to be intentional about studying Jesus' words and applying them to our hearts and lives.

In this booklet you will notice that the Scripture verses are repeated many times. Do not just skip over and move to the next page—there is value in reading and re-reading even familiar verses.

Through prayerful repetition of the words Jesus spoke to us, we can gain deeper insights into their wisdom. This practice of meditation reveals to us how alive the scripture is.

Ask God to prepare your heart to receive the knowledge He has for you. Ask Him to prepare your mind to understand how to apply the teachings. Ask also for your hands and feet to have the strength to obey. Finally, ask God for protection from confusion and doubts.

The "Remain Team" has also been praying for you. We pray that this study helps to strengthen both your convictions and your faith. We also pray that God will be glorified in any good that comes from it.

Now, let us journey together as we seek to Remain in Jesus!

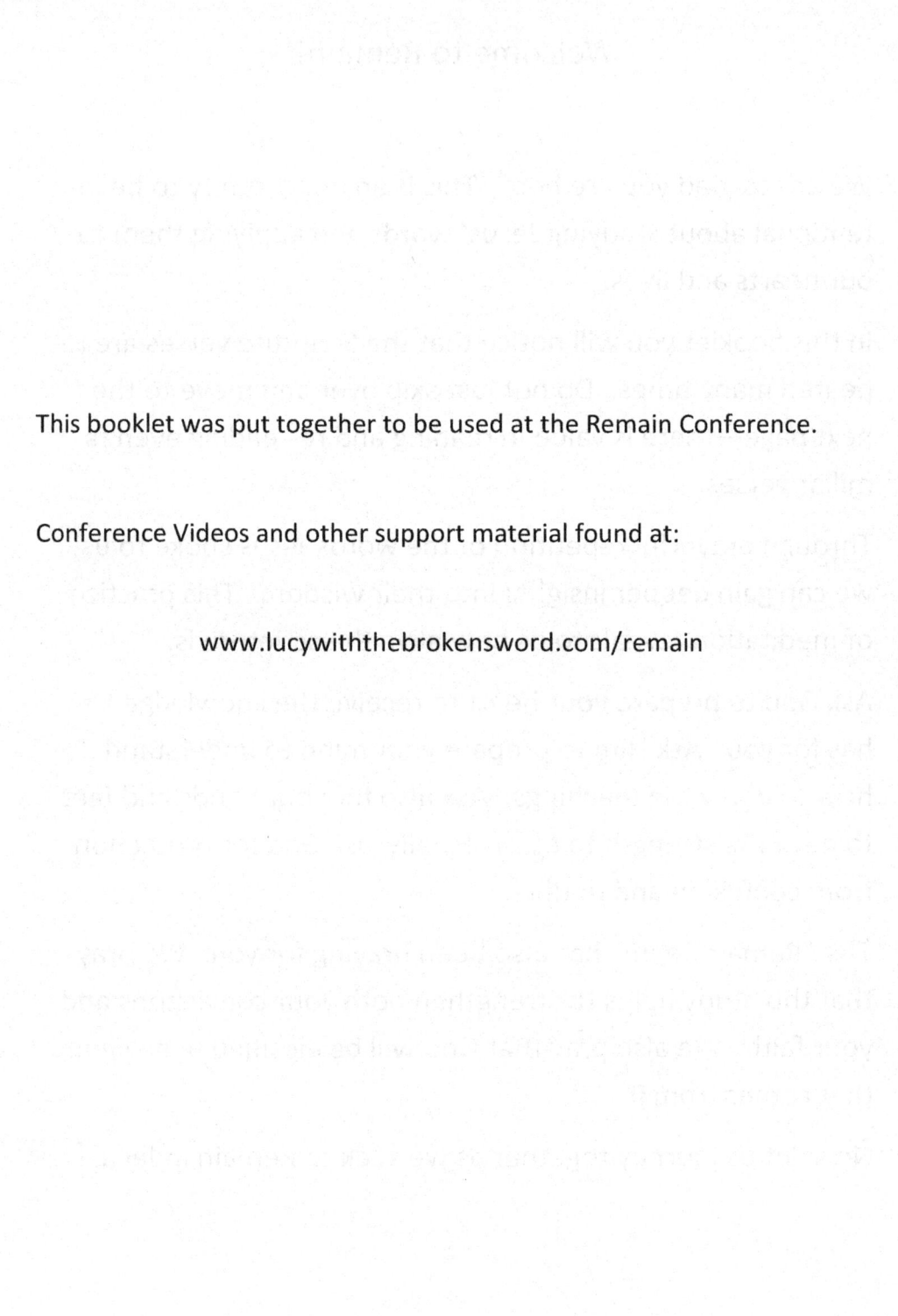

This booklet was put together to be used at the Remain Conference.

Conference Videos and other support material found at:

www.lucywiththebrokensword.com/remain

Table of Contents

- <u>Meditation Guide   page 7</u>
- <u>Introduction   page 10</u>
- <u>Section 1: Knowing the Gardener   page 16</u>

    Troubleshooting Sessions:

    ⇒ Disease: my sin nature keeps showing up_____page 22

    ⇒ Pests: worldly influence is eating away at me__page 28

    ⇒ Pruning: I need help prioritizing_____page 34

- <u>Section 2: Bearing Fruit   page 40</u>

    Troubleshooting Sessions:

    ⇒ I'm keeping busy but don't see the results____page 46

    ⇒ I feel dry and malnourished_____page 50

    ⇒ I don't know what to look for_____page 54

- <u>Section 3: Remaining in Jesus   page 58</u>

    Troubleshooting Sessions:

    ⇒ I don't know where to begin_____page 64

    ⇒ I am having trouble being consistent_____page 68

    ⇒ I keep trying to work in my own strength_____page 72

- <u>Conclusion   page 76</u>

Keep this Book of the Law always on your lips; meditate on it day and night, so that you may be careful to do everything written in it. Then you will be prosperous and successful.

-Joshua 1:8

If you remain in me and my words remain in you, ask whatever you wish, and it will be done for you.

-John 15:7

May these words of my mouth and this meditation of my heart be pleasing in your sight, Lord, my Rock and my Redeemer.

-Psalm 19:14

Techniques for Meditating Verse by Verse

- Look at specific words and think about what they mean in the context of the verse. You can even look up the definitions to give you better understanding. What does that word add to the scripture? How does the verse change if that word is changed or removed?

- By looking at the individual words, you can also glean understanding about what the scripture *doesn't* say. For example, Joshua 1:8 says, "to do *everything* written in it". The verse doesn't tell us "to do *some things* written in it". The word "everything" is an important concept we need to remember.

- Does anything in your verse remind you of another verse you've read before? Many times I use Google to help me figure out a Bible reference when I can only remember partial phrases. Joshua 1:8 reminds me of Psalm 19:14 which says, *"May these words of my mouth and this meditation of my heart be pleasing in your sight, Lord, my Rock and my Redeemer."* Finding consistent themes in scripture helps us to gain deeper knowledge of God's heart and the lessons He wants to impart to us.

- Try reading different translations to see different word choice and emphasis. What do the differences and similarities tell you about the meaning of the verse?

- Talk about it! Ask God to give you fresh perspective on His living Word. Thank Him for the verse. Also, share the verse with a friend to see what stands out to them. Joshua 1:8 says *"Keep this Book of the Law always on your lips"*, which means we should be talking about it! Scriptural insights are so valuable in our personal walk with God, however, we should share them with others when appropriate! It doesn't have to be in a preachy way—give God the glory by telling a friend how grateful you are that God has shown you something of value!

John 15:1-8 NIV

"I am the true vine, and my Father is the gardener.

He cuts off every branch in me that bears no fruit, while every branch that does bear fruit he prunes so that it will be even more fruitful.

You are already clean because of the word I have spoken to you.

Remain in me, as I also remain in you. No branch can bear fruit by itself; it must remain in the vine. Neither can you bear fruit unless you remain in me.

"I am the vine; you are the branches. If you remain in me and I in you, you will bear much fruit; apart from me you can do nothing.

If you do not remain in me, you are like a branch that is thrown away and withers; such branches are picked up, thrown into the fire and burned.

If you remain in me and my words remain in you, ask whatever you wish, and it will be done for you.

This is to my Father's glory, that you bear much fruit, showing yourselves to be my disciples."

John 15:1-8 KJV

"I am the true vine, and My Father is the vinedresser.

Every branch in Me that does not bear fruit He takes away; and every *branch* that bears fruit He prunes, that it may bear more fruit.

You are already clean because of the word which I have spoken to you.

Abide in Me, and I in you. As the branch cannot bear fruit of itself, unless it abides in the vine, neither can you, unless you abide in Me.

"I am the vine, you *are* the branches. He who abides in Me, and I in him, bears much fruit; for without Me you can do nothing.

If anyone does not abide in Me, he is cast out as a branch and is withered; and they gather them and throw *them* into the fire, and they are burned.

If you abide in Me, and My words abide in you, you will ask what you desire, and it shall be done for you.

By this My Father is glorified, that you bear much fruit; so you will be My disciples."

Introduction

"The Vine and the Branches" is a well-known passage of Scripture. But what makes the passage so significant and special? What can we learn from it and apply to our lives? The complexity of God is so vast, and so far beyond our understanding, that Jesus chose to communicate deep truths in simple terms we can more easily understand. I am so grateful that He did!

John 15 begins with an introduction: Jesus as the True Vine, and God as the Gardener. The passage later introduces *us* as Branches. From other verses, we can also ascertain that we bear fruit through the help of the Holy Spirit. So we have a Gardener, a Vine, Branches, and Fruit creating a picture of relationship and hierarchy. Once we begin to grasp our place, and our value, in the relational equation, we can appreciate all the other roles more deeply too.

Taking the roles and hierarchy lesson further, Jesus reminds us that apart from Him we can do nothing. What is the biggest difference between a Vine and a Branch? Access to the roots! A branch needs to be attached to the vine in order to benefit from the nutrients drawn through it. There is no life for a separated branch. Similarly, without Jesus, there is a gap between us and God. We must be connected to Jesus in order to bridge that separation and allow us to commune with our Creator.

Jesus wants us to grow in the way we were designed to grow. He wants us to bear fruit for His Father's glory. Yet, He doesn't command us to grow, and He doesn't command us to bear fruit. He commands us to "remain". He is confident that if we remain in Him then His nature flowing through us will result in growth and fruit. So our job is not to try to grow or produce fruit on our own strength, but simply to remain in Jesus so that the relationship and hierarchy remains intact and working.

Walking into a garden, we can be amazed by its beauty and design. We can rest in its peacefulness, and we can enjoy the buzz of life all around. However, when we take the time to observe all of the intricacies and nuances of "garden life", we can learn so much! Reading John 15, and walking quickly through the garden to the other side is fine. We can appreciate it. But when we slow down, sit in the garden for a while, and notice the details, we will marvel at the creativity and wisdom of the Gardener...

Focal Points

Relationship	How it all fits together for a greater purpose
Jesus bridges the gap between us and God—allowing us access to the roots of salvation	**Roots**
Remain	The command given to us so that we grow in the way we were designed to grow

Notes: Introduction

Reflection Time: Introduction

1. What is one question you would like God to answer during this study? It could be something you'd like wisdom for, clarity on, practical application, etc.

2. Why do you want to better understand how to "remain"?

3. What do you think hinders you from reaching the depth and consistency of relationship that you desire?

4. Choose a verse from John 15:1-8 to meditate on over the next week. Ask God to transform your understanding of it and show you the life in it.

Section 1: Knowing the Gardener

John 15:1-8 NIV

"I am the true vine, and **my Father is the gardener**.

He cuts off every branch in me that bears no fruit, while every branch that does bear fruit **he prunes** so that it will be even more fruitful.

You are already clean because of the word I have spoken to you.

Remain in me, as I also remain in you. No branch can bear fruit by itself; it must remain in the vine. Neither can you bear fruit unless you remain in me.

"I am the vine; you are the branches. If you remain in me and I in you, you will bear much fruit; apart from me you can do nothing.

If you do not remain in me, you are like a branch that is thrown away and withers; such branches are picked up, thrown into the fire and burned.

If you remain in me and my words remain in you, ask whatever you wish, and it will be done for you.

This is to my Father's glory, that you bear much fruit, showing yourselves to be my disciples."

Notes

Section 1: Knowing the Gardener

A good gardener works in his garden. A good gardener has a plan, and the authority to implement his plan. And a good gardener admires and appreciates what he has grown.

God is a good Gardener! He works in our lives and in the world around us. He has a plan for each of us, as part of a plan to maximize His glory. He has authority and dominion over everything—it is all His. And He sees that what He has made is good.

If we want to consistently remain in Jesus, and bear spiritual fruit, it is imperative that we recognize who God is. When we lose sight of that, we lose our desire and will to remain. We may be tempted to adopt a worldly view of "what's the point?", and begin to live just for ourselves.

"The Son is the image of the invisible God, the firstborn over all creation. For in Him all things were created: things in Heaven and on earth, visible and invisible, whether thrones or powers or rulers or authorities; all things have been created through Him and for Him. He is before all things, and in Him all things hold together." -**Colossians 1:15-17**

Everything was created by and for the Lord. Each of *us* were created by and for the Lord. This is both humbling and encouraging. Humbling because we are not in control, but encouraging because He knows every detail about us!

We are mere branches, and yet we are privileged to bear fruit to showcase the Gardener's glory. We should consider it an honor to be a part of the garden, and to grow in the way we were designed to grow. So we need to be focused on keeping our connection to Jesus healthy and strong. Our branch will not grow if we disconnect from Him.

With God as the Gardener, we should recognize...

...His authority.

Are you surrendering all parts of your life to Him?

...His work in our lives.

Are you allowing Him to work, or are you resisting?

...His glory.

Are you striving for Him to be glorified in every situation?

When we remember God's authority, and that everything is for Him, we will more quickly remember that He can and will help us. He wants us to be a healthy branch, remaining in Jesus, so it is okay to ask Him for help! As long as there is sin in the world, there will always be things that threaten our connection to Jesus. It is important for us to call on the Gardener so that He can work, heal, and be glorified.

In this next section, choose which "troubleshooting" topic applies best to your current walk.

Troubleshooting: Call the Gardener!

◊ Disease—my sin nature keeps showing up............page 22

◊ Pests—worldly influence is eating away at me........page 28

◊ Pruning—I need help prioritizing............page 34

Troubleshooting: Call the Gardener!

Disease: My sin nature keeps showing up

One of the most frustrating things in my garden is when I see my plants become diseased. I'd rather they become damaged and broken in a place, because at least the injury is limited and will not spread. Plant disease, when left unchecked and untreated, spreads not only throughout the infected plant, but to others as well. It may be very slow, but the nature of disease is to spread.

Sin in our lives is just like a plant disease. We may not even recognize we are infected at first, because initially it may not stunt our growth. Or, sometimes we do recognize we are sinning, but we think if we keep it contained it will be okay. *"I gossip, but only at work and nowhere else."* or *"I lie only about this specific thing."*

A plant deals with disease in a reactive way. First, if it was growing any flowers or fruit, the plant will begin dropping them. The plant will also stop or slow new growth. As the disease advances, the plant cannot afford to expend energy and resources on fruit and growth—once the disease gets to a certain point, the plant is simply trying to survive. It is gradual, at first. And the disease might even appear contained for a while.

If our sin disease is ignored and untreated, our entire branch will become infected. But a branch cannot cure itself. Our good and faithful Gardener knows how to deal with the sin in our lives—and He has provided the cure! Are you willing to let Him help you with your sin nature?

◊ One of the first steps towards dealing with sin is acknowledging it! Confess your sin to God, and adopt of a heart posture of repentance.

◊ Once we acknowledge what we are struggling with, we must ask God for wisdom in how to overcome it in the future.

◊ Remember that Jesus died for each and every one of your sins. When you are tempted to repeat the offense, ask yourself if the pleasure gained is worth spilling more of Jesus' blood.

Reflection Time:

1. What sin would you say that you struggle with the most right now? What is motivating you to address it?

2. Identify what it is that makes the sin appealing and repeatable. What are you getting out of it? Approval from others, vindication, pleasure, stress-relief, accomplishment of your own will, etc. Ask God to help you replace the draw of sin, with a draw towards Him.

3. 1 Corinthians 10:13 says that, "No temptation has overtaken you except what is common to mankind. And God is faithful; He will not let you be tempted beyond what you can bear. But when you are tempted, he will also provide a way out so that you can endure it." What tool has God given you to help you endure?

(cont.)

4. Fill out the next page and cut it out. Put it on your mirror, steering wheel, kitchen sink window, or wherever you need it to remind yourself to stand firm against the temptation to sin.

5. Remember: The war is already won. The Gardener already has the cure for the disease of sin that threatens to separate us from Him. We must claim the victory by remembering the sacrifice made for us. And we must honor the sacrifice Jesus made, by choosing Him above our sinful desires.

Remain:

Sin to overcome: _____

Replacing it with: _____

Motivation to stand firm: _____
_____

Scripture to meditate on: _____
_____
_____
_____
_____

Accountability partner: _____

For Inspiration and Meditation

"Be alert and of sober mind. Your enemy the devil prowls around like a roaring lion looking for someone to devour. Resist him, standing firm in the faith, because you know that the family of believers throughout the world is undergoing the same kind of sufferings. And the God of all grace, who called you to his eternal glory in Christ, after you have suffered a little while, will himself restore you and make you strong, firm and steadfast. To him be the power for ever and ever. Amen" **-1 Peter 5:8-11**

"She will give birth to a son, and you are to give him the name Jesus, because he will save his people from their sins." **-Matthew 1:21**

"Therefore, there is now no condemnation for those who are in Christ Jesus, because through Christ Jesus the law of the Spirit who gives life has set you free from the law of sin and death. For what the law was powerless to do because it was weakened by the flesh, God did by sending his own Son in the likeness of sinful flesh to be a sin offering. And so he condemned sin in the flesh, in order that the righteous requirement of the law might be fully met in us, who do not live according to the flesh but according to the Spirit." **-Romans 8:1-4**

"If we claim to be without sin, we deceive ourselves and the truth is not in us. If we confess our sins, he is faithful and just and will forgive us our sins and purify us from all unrighteousness. If we claim we have not sinned, we make him out to be a liar and his word is not in us." **-1 John 1:8-10**

"Have mercy on me, O God, according to your unfailing love; according to your great compassion blot out my transgressions. Wash away all my iniquity and cleanse me from my sin." **-Psalm 51:1-2**

Troubleshooting: Call the Gardener!

Pests: Worldly influence is eating away at me

Sometimes my plants can be growing well: lush leaves, beautiful flowers, ripening fruit, etc. But then I'll come outside in the morning and see a lot of damage! It's amazing how quickly a caterpillar can eat all the leaves on a stem; the branch suddenly looking naked and bare. When I'm looking through my garden, I always see *evidence* of pests before I see the actual culprit. Leaves that have vanished, holes in fruit, silky residue left behind, and even caterpillar poop!

When I see this evidence, I have to stop whatever other gardening task I had set out to do, and hunt. Occasionally, the caterpillar or other pest is easily spotted because they contrast with the plant color they are on. However, most of the time they are camouflaged and cleverly hidden. Following the trail of evidence, I eventually find the insect and remove it.

Worldly influence can eat away at our growth just as stealthily. Things like TV shows, music, gossip, commercials, and even the opinions of friends, can consume us if we are not careful. We often don't notice the consequences right away; caterpillars are very small when they first start eating a plant. But the longer they are allowed to remain, the larger they become and the more damage they do.

When we begin to recognize damage in our hearts, like maybe we are getting less and less patient, or maybe our peace is being stolen, then we need to go caterpillar hunting! And just like in nature, sometimes the pests are obvious because they stand in stark contrast to who we are. But sometimes we need to look very closely at ourselves to determine what is influencing us in a negative way.

Paul gives us some good advice in Philippians 4:8: "Finally, brothers and sisters, whatever is true, whatever is noble, whatever is right, whatever is pure, whatever is lovely, whatever is admirable—if anything is excellent or praiseworthy—think about such things." This is a good list for us to test things against as we hunt for caterpillars in our hearts.

Reflection Time:

1. Is there evidence of worldly pests in your heart? Mindsets that are in opposition to the fruits of the spirit are often indications that we are allowing ungodly influence in our lives. Anxiety, anger, selfishness, impatience, etc. are exacerbated by what we are surrounded with. Ask God to reveal to you the area He would have you address.

2. Think about the things that influence your mind and heart—how do you act after you are around them? For example, after you are around certain people are you more anxious? Or maybe a TV show is creating callousness in your heart. Or perhaps that social media feed eats away at the gratitude you have. What is an influence that you need to block or set boundaries with?

3. Psalm 51:10 says, "Create in me a pure heart, O God, and renew a steadfast spirit within me." God is faithful to help us remove, and protect us from, the things of this world. But sometimes, we do not want His help. Sometimes we are unwilling to let Him remove a caterpillar, even though we know it is only causing damage. Ask Him to help you stop idolizing the pest, and surrender to Him instead.

4. Fill out the next page and cut it out. Put it on your mirror, steering wheel, kitchen sink window, or wherever you need to remind yourself that you are choosing things of God over the things of this world.

5. Remember: If we are remaining in Jesus, surrounded by Him and His influence, we are protected from those spiritual caterpillars that try to stunt our growth and distract us from glorifying God.

Remain:

Influence to block/set boundaries with: _____

_____

Replacing it with:_____

Motivation to stand firm:_____

_____

Scripture to meditate on:_____

_____

_____

_____

_____

Accountability partner:_____

For Inspiration and Meditation

"My prayer is not that you take them out of the world but that you protect them from the evil one. They are not of the world, even as I am not of it. Sanctify them by the truth; your word is truth." **-John 17:15-17**

"As iron sharpens iron, so one person sharpens another." **-Proverbs 27:17**

"The eye is the lamp of the body. If your eyes are healthy, your whole body will be full of light. But if your eyes are unhealthy, your whole body will be full of darkness. If then the light within you is darkness, how great is that darkness!" **-Matthew 6:22-23**

"Whoever dwells in the shelter of the Most High will rest in the shadow of the Almighty. I will say of the Lord, "He is my refuge and my fortress, my God, in whom I trust." Surely he will save you from the fowler's snare and from the deadly pestilence. He will cover you with his feathers, and under his wings you will find refuge; his faithfulness will be your shield and rampart." **-Psalm 91:1-4**

Troubleshooting: Call the Gardener!

Pruning: I need help prioritizing

In English we have expressions like, "I'm spread too thin" or "This is a fruitless endeavor". We often recognize the feeling of unproductivity, but sometimes struggle to fix the problem. Or sometimes, we find ourselves doing something we think is good, but God unexpectedly closes a door or removes the opportunity from us.

If we are spiritual branches, growing from the Vine that is Jesus, then pruning is inevitable. It is necessary. And it is healthy! God, the gentle and good Gardener, will prune us, but will we welcome it or fear it?

We want to glorify God as much as possible with our lives, and produce beautiful fruit that showcases His work. But some parts of our lives are not fruitful and they take energy away from the parts that are! These things may be obvious to us, or not. Either way, we should get into the habit of asking God to reveal what He would have us hold out for Him to cut off.

But remember, John 15:2 reminds us that God also prunes fruitful branches. If a gardener is going to prune healthy branches that are bearing fruit, he must be confident that the plant will regrow and bear even more fruit. That it is for the plant's good, and the gardener's glory… God is confident that we have the capability to go from pruned, to reinvigorated and full of life. He has confidence in the nature of His True Vine: that branches who remain connected to that True Vine will grow according to the Spirit flowing from the Vine into the branch.

To help us become more accustomed to, and open to, the pruning process, we can ask God for help with the following:

◊ Ask Him to help you surrender all parts of your life, so that if or when they are pruned, you are prepared to find your comfort in Jesus.

◊ Ask Him to show you His priorities in your life, so that you can be fruitfully focused in those areas.

◊ Ask Him to bless your obedience and growth to glorify Him.

Reflection Time:

1. Can you think of any unproductive or unfruitful areas in your life? Are they unproductive and unfruitful because you have not been bringing Jesus into them? Or are they areas you need to hold out for God's pruning shears to snip off?

2. What godly priorities do you already know about for your life? Sometimes looking at it from a simple angle will help us to prioritize. We know He has called us to love one another, to tell the truth, surrender everything to Him, not judge others, etc. When we can learn to be obedient in all situations and all things, we *are* following God's priorities for our lives, even if we don't know all the details to where He is leading us.

3. Do you get overwhelmed with all the choices in your life? All of the distractions, opportunities, responsibilities, etc. can easily cause us to have a lack of focus. But bearing spiritual fruit takes focus. It takes intentional connection to Jesus, so that the Holy Spirit flows through us. What things in your life are trying to divert your energy away from Jesus and towards fruitless endeavors?

4. Fill out the next page and cut it out. Put it on your mirror, steering wheel, kitchen sink window, or wherever you need to remind yourself that you are allowing God to prune so that you become even more fruitful.

5. Remember: Pruning is humbling. But it is a good reminder that our growth does not actually belong to us. It is for God's glory. Our concern is to stay focused on our connection to, and relationship with, Jesus. Growth and fruit will come from that connection. The cut is not meant to cause pain, it is meant to prioritize. It is meant to redirect our focus and energies towards God's priorities for us.

Remain

Area to allow God to prune: _____

_____

Replacing it with: _____

Motivation to stand firm: _____

_____

Scripture to meditate on: _____

_____
_____
_____
_____

Accountability partner: _____

For Inspiration and Meditation

"So do not fear, for I am with you; do not be dismayed, for I am your God. I will strengthen you and help you; I will uphold you with my righteous right hand." **-Isaiah 41:10**

"But seek first his kingdom and his righteousness, and all these things will be given to you as well." **-Matthew 6:33**

"You shall have no other gods before me." **-Exodus 20:3**

"Jesus replied: "'Love the Lord your God will all your heart and with all your soul and with all your mind.' This is the first and greatest commandment. And the second is like it: 'Love your neighbor as yourself.' All the Law and the Prophets hang on these two commandments." **-Matthew 22:37-40**

"For you were once darkness, but now you are light in the Lord. Live as children of light (for the fruit of the light consists of all goodness, righteousness and truth) and find out what pleases the Lord. Have nothing to do with the fruitless deeds of darkness, but rather expose them." **-Ephesians 5:8-11**

Section 2: Bearing Fruit

John 15:1-8 NIV

"I am the true vine, and my Father is the gardener.

He cuts off every branch in me that **bears no fruit**, while every branch that does bear fruit he prunes so that it will be even more **fruitful**.

You are already clean because of the word I have spoken to you.

Remain in me, as I also remain in you. No branch can **bear fruit** by itself; it must remain in the vine. Neither can you **bear fruit** unless you remain in me.

"I am the vine; you are the branches. If you remain in me and I in you, **you will bear much fruit**; apart from me you can do nothing.

If you do not remain in me, you are like a branch that is thrown away and withers; such branches are picked up, thrown into the fire and burned.

If you remain in me and my words remain in you, ask whatever you wish, and it will be done for you.

This is to my Father's glory, **that you bear much fruit**, showing yourselves to be my disciples."

Notes

Section 2: Bearing Fruit

The Vine, and its' branches, are designed to produce fruit. But what is this fruit that Jesus is talking about in John 15?

A fruit carries a copy of the seed (or many copies of the seed) that the plant has grown from. The seeds are not the original—they are copies. Similarly, people were created in the image of God. We are not the original—we copy different aspects of who He is. When God told mankind, in the Old Testament, to "be fruitful and multiply", He was asking us to duplicate His image.

The "fruitful" found in the New Testament refers to a different type of multiplication we are called to: multiplication of the works of the Spirit. When we stay connected to Jesus, we produce fruit as a result of that connection: the fruit of the Spirit! Just as a branch disconnected from the vine cannot produce its intended fruit, Jesus reminds us that we cannot produce our intended fruit if we are disconnected from Him. We must remain in Him.

This fruit, since it is a duplication of God's glorious characteristics, showcases His glory, not ours! For His glory, we bear fruit through the Spirit's work in our lives.

So if we are to produce love, joy, peace, patience, kindness, goodness, faithfulness, gentleness, and self-control then we must be receiving the spiritual nutrients necessary for those things to grow in and from us. Which means that Jesus, who is growing from God, must be planted in those things. Which means, that if He is planted in love, joy, peace, patience, kindness, goodness, faithfulness, gentleness, and self-control, then those all must be characteristics of God. Because He is planted in, and growing from, God the Father.

But we should remember that a branch does not consume its own fruit—it is grown for the Gardener! Our ultimate goal should be to focus on our connection to Jesus, so that fruit is naturally produced. Obsessing over results, or hungering after fruit, will stunt our growth and make us more vulnerable to the attacks of the enemy.

Fruit is...

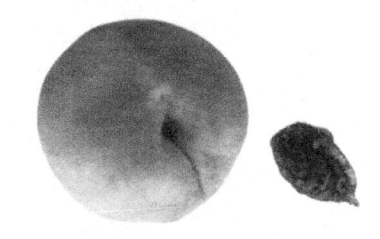

...evidence of Jesus in us.

Are you duplicating His image?

...love, joy, peace, patience, kindness, goodness, faithfulness, gentleness, and self-control.

Are these fruits growing in your heart?

...designed for the Gardener's enjoyment, not the branch's.

Are you hungry for fruit, or for what Jesus provides?

The fruits that we produce are reflections of God in our lives. They are evidence that we are growing from Him. But if we do not remain in Jesus, we will no longer reflect God's image. We will no longer produce His fruit. Jesus warned us of this, so we should make sure there is evidence of fruit on our branch!

"He cuts off every branch in me that bears no fruit, while every branch that does bear fruit he prunes, so that it will be even more fruitful." -John 15:2

In this next section, choose which "troubleshooting" topic applies best to your current walk.

Troubleshooting: Where's the Fruit?

◊ I'm keeping busy, but don't see the results............page 46

◊ I feel dry and malnourished...........page 50

◊ I don't know what to look for............page 54

Troubleshooting: Where's the Fruit?

I'm keeping busy, but don't see the results!

Isn't it frustrating when we work really hard at something, but then don't see the results we were hoping for? Or maybe progress is so slow that it feels like we aren't actually making any? If you are spinning your spiritual wheels, and not seeing fruit, then it's time to pause and evaluate.

Are you looking at the wrong branch? Maybe you've been praying and hoping for something in someone else's life, but that thing hasn't come to pass! Don't assume that there has been no fruit just because you don't see any on *their* branch—look at your own! Have you developed more patience during the process? Gentleness in the way you treat that person? Peace in knowing that God will be faithful in the circumstance? That's fruit!

Or maybe you *are* looking at yourself, and do not feel you've been producing any fruit. Maybe all of your efforts just keep looking like failure. But evaluate honestly: is it failure from a human perspective, or from God's? If you have been obedient and faithful, then that is success from God's viewpoint and there is fruit! When we try to force our own expectations onto the results of our obedience, then we are often disappointed and therefore don't see the actual fruit that is being produced!

Yet, if we have not been obedient in an area, and are not acting upon our convictions, then we will not see that kind of fruit because we won't be producing it! Disobedience leads to a disruption in the flow of spiritual nutrients we are receiving from the Vine. We can keep ourselves very busy doing "good" things, but unless we do the "right" thing that God has called us to, our growth will be stunted.

By inviting Jesus to help evaluate our heart and circumstance, we can begin to recognize the fruit that we didn't notice before, or the reasons that fruit isn't growing. Ask Him to open your spiritual eyes to help you see what needs to be seen.

Reflection Time:

1. Why do you think you aren't seeing the fruit you had hoped to see? Where are you looking? What are you looking for?

2. Is there something you've been called to do but haven't done it yet? Both a conviction to serve, and a conviction to address sin, can stunt our growth if we do not move forward in obedience. Ask Jesus to reveal what might be blocking the flow of His fruitful work in you.

3. Is there a time in your life where you saw a lot of fruit? What is different about now versus then?

(cont.)

4. What is keeping you "spiritually busy"? Are you making time to nurture a relationship with Jesus, or just checking things off of a to do list? Are you *trying* to produce fruit, or are you letting it grow naturally as you spend time with Jesus and His Word?

5. Remember: It may not always look like we think, but as surely as Jesus is Jesus, when we remain in Him, fruit will naturally grow. If your connection to Him is healthy, then ask Him to show you the fruit that you've been unable to recognize. And if you are instead convicted towards obedience, obey without delay! Fruit will follow.

For Inspiration and Meditation

"What good is it, my brothers and sisters, if someone claims to have faith but has no deeds? Can such faith save them?" **James 2:14**

"Nehemiah said, "Go and enjoy choice food and sweet drinks, and send some to those who have nothing prepared. This day is holy to our Lord. Do not grieve, for the joy of the Lord is your strength." -**Nehemiah 8:10**

"And now, dear lady, I am not writing you a new command but one we have had from the beginning. I ask that we love one another. And this is love: that we walk in obedience to his commands. As you have heard from the beginning, his command is that you walk in love." -**2 John 1:5-6**

"If after all this you will not listen to me, I will punish you for your sins seven times over. (verse 20) Your strength will be spent in vain, because your soil will not yield its crops, nor will the trees of your land yield their fruit." -**Leviticus 26:18, 20**

"Unless the Lord builds the house, the builders labor in vain. Unless the Lord watches over the city, the guards stand watch in vain." -**Psalm 127:1**

Troubleshooting: Where's the Fruit?

I feel dry and malnourished

A branch that isn't getting the proper water or nutrients won't be producing much fruit! Similarly, if we've allowed ourselves to get to a point where we feel like we've got nothing besides the bare minimum to survive, we won't produce much fruit either.

If you are feeling dry and malnourished spiritually, it is important to remember that Jesus hasn't changed. He hasn't cut you off. He is still a Vine flowing with everything we need, but if our connection to that vine has been compromised, then that flow of spiritual nutrients will have been compromised too. For example, if we are not allowing Him to penetrate all the areas of our lives, we won't be receiving everything we need to flourish and thrive. We won't be living up to our fruit-bearing potential, and we will probably feel very drained and "blah".

Jesus said, in John 7:37-38, "Let anyone who is thirsty come to me and drink. Whoever believes in me, as Scripture has said, rivers of living water will flow from within them." Are you coming to Jesus with the challenges you face? Are you believing in Him through these draining circumstances? Are you making a conscious effort to remain in Him, despite your feelings?

If we are dry or malnourished, there is hope! There is Living Water accessible to us. The Bread of Life is near to us. But we have to make the decision to eat and drink. We have to make the effort to go to Jesus, remain in Jesus, and follow Jesus. If all we do is pour ourselves out for others, or if we turn up our nose at the spiritual meal that is given to us through Jesus, then we will be weak, stagnant in our growth, and vulnerable.

Choose to go to Jesus, and then grow in Him. Even if the only thing you have energy for is to cry to Him, do it. Reestablish that connection to the Vine, so that you can become a fruit-bearing branch.

"Taste and see that the Lord is good; blessed is the one who takes refuge in Him." -Psalm 34:8

Reflection Time:

1. When did you begin to feel so spiritually dry and malnourished? Did it happen quickly, or over time? Was there a specific event or trauma that triggered this feeling?

2. What is your motivation to become spiritually healthy? Why do you care about your fruit production, or lack thereof? Ask God to help you remember why, and thank Him for His patient and faithful love.

3. How do you feel your relationship with Jesus is right now? Is it life-giving, or just kind of tired? If you were in human marriage counseling, what do you think the counsellor would recommend? Work on communication, spend more time together, rebuild trust, etc.

(cont.)

4. Use your answer from #3 to help you figure out a game plan. What is something practical that you can do this week to work on your relationship with Jesus? Do it, so that your connection to the Vine can become healthy and productive again!

5. Remember: God is a God of redemption. Even these spiritually dry seasons can be used for His glory, and they can also produce fruit! Some of the sweetest and most prized fruits take a long time to grow, fill out, and ripen. Don't lose heart in the process!

For Inspiration and Meditation

"On the last and greatest day of the festival, Jesus stood and said in a loud voice, "Let anyone who is thirsty come to me and drink. Whoever believes in me, as Scripture has said, rivers of living water will flow from within them." - **John 7:37-38**

"The Lord is near to all who call on him, to all you call on him in truth. He fulfills the desires of those who fear him; he hears their cry and saves them." - **Psalm 145:18-19**

"The Lord is close to the brokenhearted and saves those who are crushed in spirit." **-Psalm 34:18**

"Do you not know? Have you not heard? The Lord is the everlasting God, the Creator of the ends of the earth. He will not grow tired or weary, and his understanding no one can fathom. He gives strength to the weary and increases the power of the weak. Even youths grow tired and weary, and young men stumble and fall; but those who hope in the Lord will renew their strength. They will soar on wings like eagles; they will run and not grow weary, they will talk and not be faint." **-Isaiah 40:28-31**

Troubleshooting: Where's the Fruit?

I don't know what to look for

Our focus should never be solely on our fruit production, however, it is important to be able to recognize fruit! Being able to see the fruit helps encourage and motivate us, but it also helps us determine our health. If we see the fruit of the Spirit, then we can be confident that the Spirit is working in us, and we are remaining in Jesus. However, if our branch is looking pretty bare in some areas, then we need to check that connection!

But what does that fruit look like? Galatians 5 tells us that the fruits of the spirit are: love, joy, peace, patience, kindness, goodness, faithfulness, gentleness, and self-control. It almost seems too simple! This list does not line up with man's concepts of success.

It can be tempting to look at our accomplishments, especially the ones done at church or in service to others, and call those things "fruit". However, those actions themselves are not fruit. The fruits of the Spirit are hidden in our hearts, and we see evidence of them in our actions. If we only look at our actions, and not our hearts, we can deceive ourselves into thinking there is fruit when there is not.

We must continually check our hearts, to make sure that our motives are stemming from love, joy, peace, patience, kindness, goodness, faithfulness, gentleness, and self-control. These "heart checks" can show us if we are growing fruit, and they can also help us to be more intentional about learning from Jesus' example. He hasn't asked us to do anything that He did not do.

To perform a "heart check", do the following:

◊ Ask yourself why you have done the things you have done lately. Ask God to reveal your true motives so you can see if it's fruit or flesh that is behind your actions.

◊ Recite the fruits of the Spirit, pausing at each one. When was the last time you saw that fruit in your life?

◊ Ask Jesus to show you how He would handle each situation you are in.

Reflection Time:

1. Do you have the fruits of the Spirit memorized? If not, get it done! If you can't remember what to look for, then you won't recognize fruit, or lack of fruit.

2. Which fruits are very evident in your life? Think about how they have grown—was it through refinement by trials? Was it because you had someone leading by example? How can you use that successful growth to encourage you in areas you aren't as strong?

3. Which fruits seem more difficult for you to grow? Ask Jesus to show you how to remain in Him so that you can glorify God in new ways.

(cont.)

4. Are you waiting to do something because it's not yet time, or are you afraid to act and calling it patience? Are you helping someone out of true love, or enabling them, "spoiling" them, and calling it love? Are you truly joyful because of your relationship with the Lord, or are you happy in your circumstances and calling it joy? Beware of fake fruit in your life; check your heart regularly to make sure that what you are growing is from the Spirit in you and not the flesh.

5. Remember: We should not tire ourselves, or obsess over, finding fruit. Our focus and goal is to remain in Jesus. That should be our priority. When we are staying connected to Him, then the Spirit will flow through us and grow fruit. The fruit will happen not because of who we are, but who He is in us.

For Inspiration and Meditation

"But the Lord said to Samuel, "Do not consider his appearance or his height, for I have rejected him. The Lord does not look at the things people look at. People look at the outward appearance, but the Lord looks at the heart."
-1 Samuel 16:7

"If you follow my decrees and are careful to obey my commands, I will send you rain in its season, and the ground will yield its crops and the trees their fruit." -**Leviticus 26:3-4**

"But the wisdom that comes from heaven is first of all pure; then peace-loving, considerate, submissive, full of mercy and good fruit, impartial and sincere. Peacemakers who sow in peace reap a harvest of righteousness."
-James 3:17-18

"The heart is deceitful above all things and beyond cure, who can understand it? "I the Lord search the heart and examine the mind, to reward each person according to their conduct, according to what their deeds deserve.""
-Jeremiah 17:9-10

Section 3: Remaining in Him

John 15:1-8 NIV

"I am the true vine, and my Father is the gardener.

He cuts off every branch in me that bears no fruit, while every branch that does bear fruit he prunes so that it will be even more fruitful.

You are already clean because of the word I have spoken to you.

Remain in me, as I also remain in you. No branch can bear fruit by itself; it must remain in the vine. Neither can you bear fruit unless you **remain in me.**

"I am the vine; you are the branches. If you **remain in me and I in you**, you will bear much fruit; **apart from me you can do nothing.**

If you do not **remain in me**, you are like a branch that is thrown away and withers; such branches are picked up, thrown into the fire and burned.

If you **remain in me and my words remain in you**, ask whatever you wish, and it will be done for you.

This is to my Father's glory, that you bear much fruit, showing yourselves to be my disciples."

Notes

Section 3: Remaining in Him

Jesus says "remain in me" five times in John 15:1-8! But what does it mean? How do we do it? A common Christian phrase is "ask Jesus into your heart", so we frequently talk about Jesus being in us. But being *in him* at the same time seems more elusive.

Think of an empty jar being submerged into water. Suddenly, both of these are true: the jar is in the water, and the water is in the jar. This picture reminds us that we should be immersing ourselves with the things of Jesus. Surrounding ourselves with His presence through prayer, worship, and Scripture ensures that we are remaining in Him. Otherwise, we might be just like a jar of water on the counter. After a while, without access to the source of Living Water, it gets stagnant and dusty.

Next, think of two people holding hands. As their fingers intertwine, the first hand is in the second, just as the second is in the first. This concept reminds us that we can also remain in Jesus through relationship with Him. As we walk alongside Him, inviting Him into all parts of our lives, we find that we are remaining in Him as He is in us.

Finally, imagine a plug being inserted into an outlet. The plug is in the power, and now the power is in the plug. When we are drawing our strength from Jesus, we are practicing what it means to remain in Him. When we remain connected to our spiritual source of power, then we can accomplish what Jesus tells us to accomplish.

Remaining in Jesus means surrounding ourselves with Him, being in relationship with Him, and using Him as our source of life and strength. Our bodies are vessels. As Christians, we have opened our hearts for Jesus to dwell in us. He will remain in us, but will we be disciplined enough to remain in Him?

[Jesus said]

Remain in me, as I also remain in you.

The jar is in the water, as the water is in the jar.

Are you immersing yourself in Jesus' Words, so that you are in Him as He is in you?

My hand is in his hand, as his hand is in mine.

Are you walking with Jesus as a companion and source of support?

The plug is in the power, as the power is in the plug.

Are you accessing the power and nourishment that the Holy Spirit provides through your connection with Jesus?

Once we understand what it means to remain in Jesus, we must be diligent to follow through and actually remain! However, we live in a world full of distractions, discouragements, and doubts. Let us be mindful of what Jesus says about the branches that do not remain in Him:

> *"If you do not remain in me, you are like a branch that is thrown away and withers; such branches are picked up, thrown into the fire and burned."*
>
> –John 15:6

This is not a statement of condemnation, but it is a stark reminder that if we are not remaining in the Vine, as branches should, then there is no way for us to be growing fruit to glorify God. We may as well be used as kindling, because at least there is a purpose in fuel for the fire.

Instead of allowing that to paralyze us, we should find ways to remain in Jesus! In this next section, choose which "troubleshooting" topic applies best to your current walk.

Troubleshooting: Problems with the Connection

◊ I don't know where to begin ....page 64

◊ I have trouble remaining consistent...........page 68

◊ I keep trying to work in my own strength.............page 72

Troubleshooting: Problems with the Connection

I don't know where to begin!

Do you want to practice what it means to "remain in Jesus", but the concept seems difficult to begin? Or maybe it feels overwhelming, so you never start trying? You aren't alone! It can be intimidating to start something new.

We do a lot of laundry in our house. There are many of us, and we make many messes. My children are not fond of sorting the clean clothes, and so sometimes one of them will just sit there on the floor staring at the looming pile. They either don't know how to begin, or they are so overwhelmed that they don't even want to begin. So they sit there. And the laundry sits there. Nothing gets done.

If I come over and see them in this state, they already know what I'll say. "One piece at a time." I'll encourage them to pick up one item—literally any item from the pile—and take care of it. Then one more. And another. Eventually the job gets done and they can move on to something else.

We can approach our desire to remain in Jesus the same way. One step at a time. One day at a time. One moment at a time. One habit at a time. The key is to begin. Here are some first steps that you can take, in order to build up a discipline of remaining in Jesus:

- ◊ Be choosy about what you listen to: switch your car radio to worship music only, put on the audio Bible while you cook, or even, turn off all media devices and listen for God's voice instead. Surround yourself with Jesus and things that remind you of Jesus!

- ◊ Pick a regular chore/activity and bring Jesus into it each time: pray while you drive to work, meditate on a Bible verse while you vacuum, worship each time you put laundry from the washer to dryer. Moment by moment, bring Jesus into your day as you strengthen your relationship with Him.

- ◊ Think of one thing that you need to get done, and ask Jesus to help you with it. Ask Him to be with you, guide you, smooth the path before you, etc. Then, look for more opportunities to lean on Him as your source of strength.

Reflection Time:

1. What intimidates, or prevents, you most about beginning the journey to remain in Jesus?

2. What motivates you (or should motivate you) to deepen your relationship with Him?

3. What is a habit or skill that you have successfully learned in the past? It could be a spiritual discipline, like having a thankful heart, or even a secular discipline like getting into an exercise routine. Think about what techniques you used to motivate you. Did you leave sticky notes all over your house? Did you set loud obnoxious alarms for yourself as reminders? Did you ask a friend for help? Or maybe you just kept reminding yourself of the reason you were working towards the goal. Pinpoint a method that has worked for you in the past, and apply it to your goal of remaining in Jesus!

(cont.)

4. What "baby step" from the previous page are you willing to take right now? Be sure to tell a friend to help keep you accountable!

5. Remember: God is patient with us, and extends so much grace. Be patient with yourself, and give yourself grace. Habits and disciplines take time and work, so even if you feel like you are failing—don't give up!

For Inspiration and Meditation

"You are my friends if you do what I command. I no longer call you servants, because a servant does not know his master's business. Instead, I have called you friends, for everything that I learned from my Father I have made known to you." -**John 15:14-15**

"Your word is a lamp for my feet, a light on my path. I have taken an oath and confirmed it, that I will follow your righteous laws." -**Psalm 119:105-106**

"In the beginning was the Word, and the Word was with God, and the Word was God." **-John 1:1**

Troubleshooting: Problems with the Connection

I Have Trouble Remaining Consistent

Consistency can be such an elusive discipline to master! I think few of us ever achieve enough consistency in an area where we would even consider ourselves "master" over it. There are always short-comings, distractions, changes of season, etc. to seemingly undo any progress we made in the past.

It can be disheartening! Yet, I think sometimes our discouragement comes, not from what we have been unable to achieve, but from our preconceived ideas of what success looks like. Not that we shouldn't strive for *greatness*, but sometimes we lose sight of God's *graciousness*. We also lose sight of His idea of success.

I used to think that in order to consider myself consistent in my walk with God, I had to have a dedicated "quiet time" every single day. I need a devotion book and journal, I need a Bible commentary close at hand, I should take notes, and I should be doing all this before dawn. If that's your routine, how amazing for you! For years, I struggled with a certain guilt that I could not get into a routine like that. Maybe I'd try, but I could never be consistent.

Eventually, I realized that I was trying to force myself into a mold of what I thought a strong Christian woman looked like, instead of allowing God to mold me into who He designed me to be. Have *Him* show me which habits were important for me to focus on; have *Him* teach me how to become more consistent and reliable. Because our relationship with Him, should really be centered around *Him*, right?

Instead of feeling guilty or discouraged, try to shift your approach:

◊ Ask God to convict you of the areas *He* would have you work on, instead of trying to force your own spiritual growth agenda.

◊ Think of an area, or routine, in your life where you are consistent. Not necessarily perfect, but reliable. Find a way that you can bring Jesus into that routine in order to be more consistent with Him as well.

◊ Thank God for His patience and grace!

Reflection Time:

1. What specifically makes you say that you struggle with consistency? What are your biggest stumbling blocks?

2. What do you think it would look or feel like to "remain" in Jesus more? How do you think you would respond to trials differently?

3. Who are you in the habit of texting the most? Who are the people whose calls you always answer? Those people are important to you! Communication with them is important to you. The next time you answer a text or call, ask Jesus for help remaining in Him while you communicate with the people He also loves.

(cont.)

4. What is the already consistent area of your life that you are going to bring God into this week? Maybe you are faithful to feed your family supper each day—incorporate a Bible verse or hymn into the routine! Maybe you always put your shoes on before leaving the house—each time you lace up, ask Jesus to help you have the readiness that comes with the gospel of peace! (Eph 6:15) It's okay to start small, but tell someone else your plan so that you can have accountability to help you follow through!

5. Remember: God is so gracious, and so patient, with us. Don't give up when you fail to consistently remain in Jesus. Keep practicing, and keep trying new ways to be in Him. The more you want it, and the more you think about it, the more you are already remaining in Jesus!

For Inspiration and Meditation

"Fixing our eyes on Jesus, the pioneer and perfecter of faith. For the joy set before him, he endured the cross, scorning its shame, and sat down at the right hand of the throne of God. Consider him who endured such opposition from sinners, so that you will not grow weary and lose heart." -**Hebrews 12:2-3**

"My eyes are ever on the Lord, for only he will release my feet from the snare." -**Psalm 25:15**

"Therefore, my dear brothers and sisters, stand firm. Let nothing move you. Always give yourselves fully to the work of the Lord, because you know that your labor in the Lord is not in vain." **-1 Corinthians 15:58**

"I lift up my eyes to the mountains—where does my help come from? My help comes from the Lord, the Maker of heaven and earth." **-Psalm 121:1-2**

*"Is this the kind of fast I have chosen, only a day for people to humble themselves? Is it only for bowing one's head like a reed and for lying in sackcloth and ashes? Is that what you call a fast, a day acceptable to the Lord? Is not this the kind of fasting I have chosen: to loose the chains of injustice and untie the cords of the yoke, to set the oppressed free and break every yoke? Is it not to share your food with the hungry and to provide the poor wanderer with shelter—when you see the naked, to clothe them, and not to turn away from your own flesh and blood? -**Isaiah 58:5-7**

Troubleshooting: Problems with the Connection

I Keep Trying to Work in My Own Strength

Working in your own strength again, huh? Sounds like you are someone who likes control, or at least has some fear of *not* having control! But as you've probably figured out, trying to remain in control means you aren't remaining in Jesus.

But Jesus very clearly said, "Apart from me you can do nothing". In this instance, He is talking about our ability to glorify God through bearing fruit. We will not see this spiritual growth if we remain dependent on ourselves instead of Jesus.

In our own strength, we may be able to successfully go about our daily lives, handling the grocery shopping, showing up for work, walking the dog, etc. But will these things be lifeless? Or will they lead to life, growth, and the fruit of the Holy Spirit? Will our success be because of how capable *we* are, or because of how faithful *God* is?

In order to begin the habit of remaining in Jesus, and allowing Him to be strong in our situations, we must learn how to give up that control we want to hold onto so badly. Surrender, while not usually a fun process, is such an important one if we want to remain in Jesus and not our own strength!

1. Identify something in your life that you are trying to control, instead of allowing God to let His will be done. Tell Him that you want Him to be your strength for that area.

2. Ask God to show you His faithfulness in handling that situation. Ask Him to open your eyes to see His perspective on it, so that you can adjust your approach accordingly.

3. Find a way to remind yourself that you have given this area to God, so that you aren't tempted to carry the burden again. A specific scripture, hymn, pep-talk phrase, etc. can help you to keep Jesus in the situation, as you remain in Him.

4. Repeat! Surrender that situation and find more areas to surrender!

Reflection Time:

1. What things in your life seem to sap you of your energy most? What are your biggest stresses and burdens?

2. How do you recognize that you are trying to do them in your own strength? What do you think it would look like if Jesus was carrying the load for you? How would your approach and results look different?

3. Are there any areas in your life that you easily hand over to God? Why is it easier to let God be strong in those areas, but not others? What are you afraid of happening if you give up control?

(cont.)

4. Start small. What is one specific burden in your life that you have been trying to handle, instead of trusting God to be your source of strength? Go through the process of surrendering, so that you are not excluding Jesus from that area of your life. Be sure to tell a friend to help encourage you in the process!

5. Remember: God is much greater, more powerful, and more loving than we are. We can trust Him with our burdens—small and large. Think about His past faithfulness, and let that feed your confidence in His ability to handle your current and future situations!

For Inspiration and Meditation

"Come to me, all you who are weary and burdened, and I will give you rest. Take my yoke upon you and learn from me, for I am gentle and humble in heart, and you will find rest for your souls. For my yoke is easy and burden is light."-**Matthew 11:28-30**

"Nehemiah said, "Go and enjoy choice food and sweet drinks, and send some to those who have nothing prepared. This day is holy to our Lord. Do not grieve, for the joy of the Lord is your strength." -**Nehemiah 8:10**

"But he said to me, "My grace is sufficient for you, for my power is made perfect in weakness." Therefore I will boast all the more gladly about my weaknesses, so that Christ's power may rest on me." -**2 Corinthians 12:9**

"I know what it is to be in need, and I know what it is to have plenty. I have learned the secret of being content in any and every situation, whether well fed or hungry, whether living in plenty or in want. I can do all this through him who gives me strength.." -**Philippians 4:12-13**

Conclusion

Jesus is the True Vine. His Father, God, is the Gardener. We are branches, designed to bear fruit which brings glory to God and shows the world His image. The goal for us, as branches, is to remain in Jesus so that we are being obedient and growing as we were designed. The passage, John 15:1-8, heavily emphasizes that concept of "remain", however it also gives us some other insights to help us keep perspective.

"You are already clean because of the word I have spoken to you." (verse 3) "Already clean" reminds us that our salvation comes from what Jesus did for us, not through anything we work to earn. So we can do our best to practice remaining in Jesus, and be spiritually healthy, but the "Vine & Branches" talk is not about our salvation itself.

Similarly, we can remember verse 4: "Remain in me, as I also remain in you." Jesus says, "AS", not, "SO THAT". "As" is such a valuable word in this verse because it reminds us that, just as we did nothing to earn salvation, Jesus doesn't just leave us because we choose to disobey and not remain in Him. We do not dictate where He chooses to reside, and we cannot impact or change His nature. If He says He will remain in us, then we cannot escape that. We can, however, choose to be immersed in things that are not of Him. We can choose to surround ourselves with earthly things instead of Jesus. But we do not have the authority to choose where Jesus says He will be.

Jesus also reminds us to, "Ask whatever you wish, and it will be done for you." (verse 7) It sounds great, doesn't it?! However, He prefaces this statement with, "If you remain in me, and my words remain in you". If we truly want God to honor our requests, we should be diligent about knowing what Jesus said and allowing it to overflow out of our hearts and into our requests.

Walking into a garden, we can be amazed by its beauty and design. We can rest in its peacefulness, and we can enjoy the buzz of life all around. However, when we take the time to observe all of the intricacies and nuances of "garden life", we can learn so much! Now that we have slowly read through John 15, and noticed the details, we can marvel all the more at the creativity and wisdom of the Gardener...

Let us remember these lessons, so we can remain in Jesus every day!

Final Reminders

| **Already Clean** | We did nothing to earn our salvation—it is only because of what Jesus did. |

| Jesus remains in us AS we remain in Him, not SO THAT we remain in Him. | **As** |

| **Ask** | If Jesus' words remain in us, then when we ask God for something, we will be speaking the words of Jesus. |

Notes: Conclusion

Reflection Time: Conclusion

1. Has God taught you anything during this study?

2. What verse in John 15 stood out to you the most during this study? Why?

3. What is a practical step towards strengthening your relationship with Jesus that you are excited/convicted/motivated to take?

4. In your own words, how would you describe what Jesus meant when He commanded us to "remain"?

Made in United States
North Haven, CT
04 February 2025

65398790R00046